I0147081

George Quayle Cannon

Book of Mormon Stories

Adapted to the capacity of young children, and designed for use in

Sabbath schools, Primary associations, and for home reading

George Quayle Cannon

Book of Mormon Stories
*Adapted to the capacity of young children, and designed for use in Sabbath schools,
Primary associations, and for home reading*

ISBN/EAN: 9783337298371

Printed in Europe, USA, Canada, Australia, Japan

Cover: Foto ©Lupo / pixelio.de

More available books at **www.hansebooks.com**

Book of Mormon

Stories.

NO. 1.

Illustrated.

*ADAPTED TO THE CAPACITY OF YOUNG CHILDREN,
AND DESIGNED FOR USE IN SABBATH
SCHOOLS, PRIMARY ASSOCIATIONS,
AND FOR HOME READING.*

PUBLISHED BY

GEORGE Q. CANNON & SONS CO.,

SALT LAKE CITY, UTAH.

1892.

PREFACE.

THIS little work containing Book of Mormon stories, is issued as a companion volume to the "Simple Bible Stories" series. It is written for the purpose of presenting the Book of Mormon narrative in language that can be understood by small children. It is arranged so that it can be used in connection with the Book of Mormon Chart No. 1, published by the Deseret Sunday School Union. Each picture on the Chart is made the subject of a story in this work, and the illustrations in the book are similar to those on the Chart.

THE PUBLISHERS.

CONTENTS.

LEHI AND HIS SONS.

BOOK OF MORMON STORIES.

LEHI AND HIS SONS

THE PROPHET LEHI IN JERUSALEM.

THE Bible tells about the peoples who lived a long time ago in a far off country called Asia. The city of Jerusalem is in Asia. In and around Jerusalem many of the Prophets of the Lord lived many years ago.

The Savior was born in a small town near this great city, and when He lived on the earth He went to Jerusalem several times. He also visited other towns near by to teach the people.

Jerusalem was built on a hill, and had a high wall around it, so that people could only get in and out of the city through the gates. A great many people lived there. They had many fine houses and a very beautiful temple, which was the grandest and nicest building in the world.

The Book of Mormon tells about a people who came from Jerusalem to this country where we live, which is now called America. The Indians who live among us are the children of the people whom the Book of Mormon speaks of. Their forefathers came from Jerusalem many hundreds of years ago.

At the same time when the Prophet Jeremiah, of whom the Bible tells, was living near Jerusalem, another Prophet

2

named Lehi dwelt in that great city. This was six hundred years before the Savior was born. The king who was ruler at Jerusalem at this time was named Zedekiah. He was not

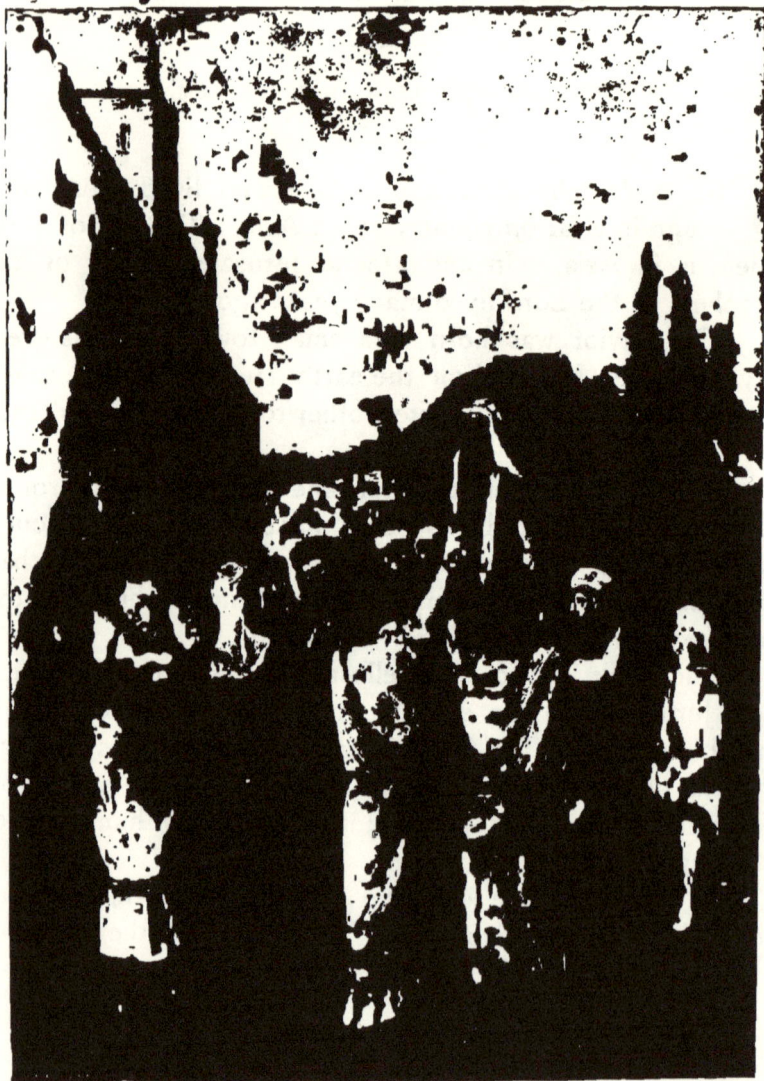

LEHI PREACHING TO THE JEWS.

a good man, and did not do as the Lord wished him to. Many of the people of the city were also wicked. Jeremiah told the king and the people of their wickedness, and that their city would be destroyed unless they lived better lives and obeyed the Lord.

The Prophet Lehi also preached to the people, and told them what awful things would happen to them because of their sins. The people did not believe Lehi, and they became angry at him because he told them of evils which would come upon them. They even tried to kill him, but the Lord did not let them harm His servant.

Both Lehi and Jeremiah told the people of Jerusalem, who were called Jews, that a king who lived in another city called Babylon would come with a great army of soldiers and destroy Jerusalem. They would tear down the walls of the city and burn the houses in which the people lived. Then these soldiers would kill many of the people who lived in the city, and others would be taken away to Babylon and put into prison. The Lord told these Prophets, Lehi and Jeremiah that these things should happen, and that is how they knew about what would happen.

The Lord loved the people of Jerusalem. Sometimes they were good people, and the Lord wanted to save them. But they had become so wicked that the Lord now sent these and many other Prophets to warn them, or tell them of what should happen if they did not do better.

The people would not do right, so, just as these Prophets had said, in a few years the king of Babylon sent a great army of soldiers to Jerusalem, and they killed many thousands of the men and women. They took others to prison, and the city and the beautiful temple were burned.

Perhaps you will wonder what became of the few good people who were in Jerusalem. The Lord took care of those who loved Him. Jeremiah was treated kindly by the king of Babylon, and was allowed to stay with a few others in his old home. Daniel, and a few other good young men whom the Bible tells of, were carried to Babylon and placed in the king's palace, where they were kindly treated. Lehi and his family and a few others were cared for in a different way. How the Lord so wonderfully provided for their safety will be told in the next story.

This story shows that the Lord is kind to His children, and tells them how to be saved from trouble, just as our parents teach us how to avoid dangers and accidents. If we obey our parents we are safe from harm; so when people obey the Lord they are safe, for He will protect them. The story teaches us, also, that what the Lord says is always the truth. He never promises to do anything and fails to do it. Another thing in this story to be remembered is that the Lord is not pleased with wicked people, and they are sure to be punished for their sins.

———

Points to be remembered in this story: Jerusalem is a city in Asia, where the Savior and many Prophets have lived long time ago—The Book of Mormon tells about a Prophet named Lehi who lived in Jerusalem many years before the Savior was born—The people at that time were wicked—Lehi told them of their sins, and that they would be destroyed if they did not do right. The people did not repent, and an army of soldiers came from Babylon and burned the city, killed many people, and took others to prison—The good people were saved—The Lord is kind to His children—He always tells the truth—He is not pleased with wicked people.

LEHI AND HIS SONS.

THEIR JOURNEY IN THE WILDERNESS.

AFTER the Prophet Lehi had warned the people of Jerusalem of what was going to happen, the Lord told him in a dream to leave the city and take his family with him.

The people did not believe what he said would take place, and they were angry with him because he told them of their sins. They wanted to kill Lehi, so the Lord told him to leave them.

Lehi had lived in Jerusalem all his life up to this time. Besides having a home he had much gold and silver and other valuable things. But he left all these and with his family journeyed in the wilderness, as the Lord commanded him. What is meant by the wilderness is a desert or land that is not cultivated; where there are no houses for people to live in. The country south of Jerusalem was generally called the wilderness, as it was rough and uncultivated. Lehi and his family traveled south from Jerusalem until they came to this wilderness.

For three days they traveled in the wilderness, when they came to a valley by the shore of the Red Sea. In this valley was a river, and they camped by its side. They brought with them provisions, food and such things as they would need, and tents to live in.

As they expected to stay here for some time they pitched their tents. Lehi built an altar here and made an offering or sacrifice to the Lord, and thanked Him for His goodness. The Lord had told him to leave Jerusalem

LEHI AND HIS FAMILY IN THE WILDERNESS.

because the people wanted to take his life and he was thankful for being saved in this way.

Lehi's wife was named Sariah.   They had four sons at

this time. The sons' names were Laman, Lemuel, Sam and Nephi. They also had daughters but their names are not told in the Book of Mormon.

The two older sons of Lehi, Laman and Lemuel, complained because their father left his house and land and all his riches and brought his family into the wilderness to die. They did not believe that Jerusalem would be destroyed; nor did they believe the Lord commanded him to leave Jerusalem for safety from the wicked people there. As they did not have faith in the Lord they were afraid they might die in the wilderness for want of food.

Nephi and Sam believed what their father had told them, and were more willing to obey him. Nephi especially had great faith in the Lord. He fully believed the Lord had spoken to his father, and he prayed to the Lord that he might know for himself the things of God which his father spoke about.

Nephi's prayers were answered. The Lord visited him and told him many wonderful things. He blessed Nephi, and said he would become the ruler of his brethren who were disobedient. The Lord also told Nephi that He would lead his father's family to a beautiful and rich country, called the Land of Promise.

The Lord is ever willing to answer prayers. Those who pray to Him for knowledge or wisdom or anything that is for their good will be sure to receive an answer, if they ask in faith, believing the Lord will hear them.

If Nephi's brothers, Laman and Lemuel had faith and prayed to the Lord they would know also that their father was a truthful man and was a prophet of God. But they were not willing to do this, and therefore they were not blest like their brother Nephi.

This story shows us that the Lord will protect and bless those who trust in Him. In the following stories about Lehi

and his family we shall see how the Lord continued to bless
them and provide for their needs, and how He led them to a

ARAB'S MODE OF TRAVELING IN THE DESERT.

tar off land that was not known to other people in the world.

Points to be remembered in this story: Lehi told in a dream to leave Jerusalem and go into the wilderness, that he and his family might be saved —They go south from Jerusalem and camp by a river near the Red Sea— Lehi's wife named Sariah, his sons named Laman, Lemuel, Sam and Nephi— Laman and Lemuel are not satisfied with their father's doings, and complain—They do not believe what he tells them—Nephi a faithful and obedient son—He prays to the Lord and receives an answer to his prayers—The Lord blesses him and tells him many things—The Lord always willing to answer prayers—The Lord protects those who trust in Him.

LEHI AND HIS SONS.

THE SONS RETURN TO JERUSALEM.

WHILE Lehi's family were living in their tents in the wilderness by the shore of the Red Sea the Lord told Lehi in a dream to send his sons back to Jerusalem.

There was a man in Jerusalem who had some plates of brass on which was written or engraved the record or history of Lehi's relatives, his father, grandfather, great-grandfather, and others. They gave an account of the Jews from the time they came to Jerusalem and for a long time before they came there. The record on the plates also told about the creation of the world, about Adam and Eve, our first parents, about Noah, and Abraham, and Moses, and many other people.

Lehi wanted these plates to take with him, that his family and those who lived with them might have an account of their forefathers, and the laws of the Lord which were given through Moses, which were also contained on these brass plates.

At the time when Lehi lived the people did not have books made of paper, like those we have. Instead of paper to write on they used skins of animals and other materials. Sometimes they used brass or gold plates, and cut the writing into the plates with a sharp knife or other tool.

Lehi sent his four sons back to Jerusalem to get these plates from Laban, the man who was taking care of them.

When Laman and Lemuel were told that they must go they again complained and found fault with their father; but when Nephi was spoken to about going he was very willing to do so and did not complain. Laman and Lemuel thought it was very hard for them to go back on such an errand, but Nephi said he knew the Lord would not want them to do anything they were not able to; and he believed the Lord would watch over them while on their journey. How much better it would have been for them all to be obedient like Nephi was will be seen from the following stories. So Nephi and his other brothers took their tents and started on their journey.

When they reached the city of Jerusalem they decided among themselves that Laman, the older one of the four, should go to Laban's house and ask for the plates. It was right that their father should have the plates, or the Lord would not have told him to send for them. But when Laman asked Laban to give the plates to him he became angry. He called Laman a robber, and said he would kill him. Laman then ran away, so the man did not catch him.

When Laman went back to where his brothers were waiting for him and told what had happened they all felt very sorry. The older brothers wanted to go back to their father; but Nephi was determined to get the plates for which he had been sent. He persuaded his brothers to stay with him, and they went to their father's old home and gathered up the gold and silver and other precious things which had been left there. These things they took to Laban and offered them to him if he would give them the brass plates that contained the writings or records.

When Laban saw they had so much gold and silver and other valuable things he wanted to get the things, but would not give up the plates. So he put Lehi's sons out of his house, then he sent his servants after them to slay them and take their property. When these servants of Laban came after Nephi and his brothers they had to leave their gold and silver and run for their lives. They got out of the city and hid in a cave or hole in a rock, and so the men who were after them could not find them.

After this Laman and Lemuel became angry with Nephi and Sam, and they whipped them with a rod. Then an angel from heaven appeared and told them to not harm their younger brother Nephi, but to go again to Laban and the Lord would help them in performing their errand. When the angel left them Laman and Lemuel again complained, and said they did not believe they could perform their errand. Nephi reasoned with them and persuaded them to go with him towards the city, although they were still dissatisfied and angry.

When they got to the gate of Jerusalem it was night. Nephi told his brothers to hide there while he crept into the city.

He went towards the house where Laban lived and on his way near the house he saw a man lying on the ground. The man was drunk. He looked at him and found it was Laban. Laban had a sword with him, which Nephi drew from its sheath. He examined it, and saw it was made of fine steel, with a beautiful handle made of pure gold.

While Laban lay before him on the ground the Spirit of

NEPHI'S RETURN WITH THE BRASS PLATES.

the Lord told Nephi to kill him.   Nephi did not like to do
this.   He was a good young man, and knew it was not right
to kill.   But the Lord commanded him to kill Laban, and he

obeyed the Lord. Nephi then put Laban's clothes on himself and went into Laban's house. Here he found the
servant who took care of Laban's treasures. Nephi told this
man to go and get the plates of brass from the place where
they were kept and follow him. The servant, whose name
was Zoram, thought it was Laban who was talking to him.
He therefore brought out the plates that contained the records
and went with Nephi to where his brothers were outside the
gates of the city.

When Laman, Lemuel and Sam saw Nephi coming they
were very much frightened. They thought he was Laban,
because he was dressed in Laban's clothes. They believed
Nephi was killed and Laban was coming to kill them. So
they began to run. Nephi called them, and they found it was
their brother and not Laban.

By this time Zoram, who was with Nephi, became frightened and was going to run back into the city, but Nephi held
him. Afterwards Nephi persuaded Zoram to go with him and
promised him they would not hurt him.

This story shows us that the Lord does not ask His
children to do anything that is impossible, or that they cannot
do. He understands all things, and knows what His children
are able to do. Nephi's doings teach us a very good lesson
in perseverance and patience. We can see how, by trying
again and not giving up, we can do things that seem impossible at first.

Points to be remembered in this story: Lehi sends his sons back to
Jerusalem to get plates that contain an account or history of their forefathers
His older sons complain, but Nephi offers to go willingly—When the sons
reach Jerusalem Laman goes to see Laban, the man who has the plates—
Laban gets angry, calls Laman a robber, and says he will kill him—Laman
runs away to save his life—The four brothers go to their father's old home
and get the gold and silver and other precious things left there and offer

them to Laban for the plates—Laban refuses to give up the plates, and sends
his servants to kill Lehi's sons and take their property—Lehi's sons escape
by hiding in a cave—They go the third time to get the plates—Nephi finds
Laban drunk—Being commanded of the Lord, Nephi kills him and gets the
plates from his servant—Nephi takes Zoram, Laban's servant, and the plates
to where his brothers are outside the city.

LEHI AND HIS SONS.

THE SONS' SECOND JOURNEY TO JERUSALEM.

WHILE Lehi's sons were away on their errand to Jerusalem to get the records, their mother was very
uneasy about them. She feared they might get killed or
might die in the wilderness. When they came back both
their father and mother were filled with joy, and were thankful to the Lord for their safe return.

Sometime after the sons' return to the place where they
camped in the wilderness, their father was told by the Lord
to send again to Jerusalem.

The Lord desired to lead Lehi and those who were with
him to a country where there were no people. There was a
man named Ishmael, living in Jerusalem who had several
sons and daughters. The Lord commanded Lehi to send for
Ishmael and invite him to go with them to the new country.

Lehi's sons were not married, and by getting Ishmael
and his family to go with them the sons of Lehi might take
Ishmael's daughters for wives. This was the reason why the
Lord desired Lehi to send for Ishmael.

Laman, Lemuel, Sam and Nephi were sent to Jerusalem
for this family. When they reached Ishmael's house they

told him what they had come for. Ishmael and his family were willing to go with them, and so they all traveled together into the wilderness.

While on their journey Nephi's two older brothers and some of Ishmael's sons and daughters rebelled against Nephi and the other members of Ishmael's family. That is, they refused to go with them. They wanted to return to Jerusalem. Nephi told them that if they did return they would be killed with the others who were there, as Jerusalem would surely be destroyed. Being blessed with the Spirit of the Lord, Nephi spoke with great power to his brethren. But this only made them angry. They became so angry that they took Nephi and bound him with cords. They wanted to kill him and leave him there in the wilderness to be eaten by wild beasts.

While Nephi was bound he prayed to the Lord to protect and save him from his wicked brothers. The Lord answered his prayers. The cords with which he was bound became loosened and he was set free.

Again, before they reached the end of their journey, Nephi's older brothers became angry and wanted to slay him. But this time Ishmael's wife and one of her sons and one daughter stopped them, and persuaded them to leave him alone.

Afterwards Laman and Lemuel felt very sorry for being so cruel to their brother. They asked him to forgive them for what they had done. Nephi at once forgave them, and was glad to see them repent of their wickedness. He loved his brothers even when they tried to take his life. Nephi told Laman and Lemuel to ask the Lord to forgive them and they did this. Then they all went on their journey and soon came to the place where Lehi and those who were with him were stopping.

This story shows again how the Lord watches over those

NEPHI'S BRETHREN SEEK HIS LIFE.

who do right, and how he keeps them from harm when the
wicked try to hurt them.   Each time when Nephi was in
danger the Lord saved him from all harm.   This was because
Nephi was a good man, and was obedient and faithful to the
Lord.   He was also obedient to his father Lehi, who loved
him very much.

Points to be remembered in this story :—Lehi's sons sent to Jerusalem
a second time—Their errand is to invite a man named Ishmael and his
family to join their father's family in the wilderness—As the Lord intended
to lead Lehi and his family to a new country where there were no people,
it was desirable that Ishmael go with them—Ishmael had several daughters,
whom it was expected would become the wives of Lehi's sons—Ishmael and
family agree to go into the wilderness—After starting Laman and Lemuel
and some of Ishmael's family rebel and want to turn back—Nephi encour-
ages them to keep on their journey—They become angry at Nephi and bind
him with cords, intending to kill him—Nephi prays and the Lord loosens
the cords and he gets free—Again Nephi's older brothers want to take his
life, but Ishmael's wife and her son and daughter stop them and persuade
them to leave him alone—Afterwards Laman and Lemuel are sorry and ask
Nephi to forgive them—Nephi forgives his brothers and they all go on their
journey and come to the place where Lehi is stopping—The Lord always
takes care of those who obey Him.

LEHI AND HIS SONS.

NEPHI'S VISION.

WHILE Lehi was in the wilderness the Lord showed him in visions many things that would happen in the world a long time afterwards. A vision is something like a dream in which a person sees things as they really are or as they will be. When a vision is from the Lord that which is shown is something that has or will really happen. The way the Lord tells His prophets about what is going to take place is often by showing them a vision or a dream in which they see what is going to happen just as it will be when it takes place.

When Lehi had these visions he told about them to his children. Nephi was so interested or pleased with what his father told him that he wanted to see the visions for himself. So he prayed often to the Lord and asked Him to show him the things that his father Lehi saw. Nephi had such strong faith that he was enabled to receive an answer to his prayers.

At one time, when Nephi was thinking about what his father had seen, a vision of the Lord came to him. In this vision he was taken up into a high mountain. An angel of the Lord spoke to him and asked him what he desired. Nephi said he wished to see what his father had seen. The angel said to Nephi "Look!" Nephi looked and he saw Jerusalem as it would appear in six hundred years to come. Then he saw other cities. In the city of Nazareth which was near Jerusalem he saw a very beautiful virgin or young woman. The angel said this was the mother of the Savior.

NEPHI'S VISION.

Soon after he looked again and saw this beautiful young woman with a child in her arms.   The angel told Nephi that the child was the Savior, and that after many years from that time He would be born and live upon the earth.   Nephi then saw the Savior grown to manhood, and He went to John the baptist to be baptized.   After this the Spirit of God, or the Holy Ghost rested upon · the Savior and He went about teaching the people the gospel, telling them how they should live.   He also healed the sick, and the blind and the lame, and raised dead persons to life.   Nephi continued to took upon the vision and he saw the Savior taken by the wicked people and nailed to a cross and left there to die.   The angel explained to Nephi that in this way the Savior would die for the sins of the world.

Afterwards appeared the Savior's apostles and then he saw that the wicked people in the world fought against the church the Savior started on the earth, and killed the saints who belonged to the church; then the people in the world were left for a long time without the gospel.

Many other things that have happened in the world since that time were seen by Nephi.   He also saw things that have happened in this time when we live.

All the things which Nephi saw in this great vision came to pass just as he saw them many hundreds of years before. The Savior was born six hundred years after Nephi saw Him in this vision.   His mother lived in the city of Nazareth where Nephi saw her.   The Savior was baptized and went about teaching the people, healing the sick, the blind and the lame, and raising the dead.   He was crucified, too, just as Nephi saw He would be; and the church which He started was destroyed on the earth, the saints being lput to death by wicked men.

From this story we may learn that the Lord knows all about what will happen in this world.   He knew before the world was made what would take place in the thousands of years to come. The Lord knows all things. He knows what each one of us may do or say. He even knows what we think, when we do not act or speak. When we say or do anything that is not right He knows about it, and is displeased. When we do good He sees it, and is pleased with us. If we try always to do right He will love us and will help us to do good.

We learn also from this story that the Lord tells good men about many things that are going to take place before they do happen. This is because He loves them.

By knowing what is going to happen beforehand these good men can often save themselves from danger or trouble.

In this way Lehi and his family were saved from death by leaving Jerusalem before it was destroyed. Lehi tried also to save the people of Jerusalem by telling them what was going to happen, but they would not believe him. They were so wicked they tried to kill him, and he had to leave to save his own life.

———

Points to be remembered in this story.   Lehi sees many things in visions—He tells about them to his family—Nephi so pleased with hearing what his father tells he desires to see the things himself—An angel shows him a beautiful vision in which he sees the Savior and His mother—He also sees the Savior teaching the people and healing the sick—Sees Him nailed to a cross—Sees what happens afterwards—His church destroyed—The Lord knows all things—He tell His prophets many things that are going to take place.

LEHI AND HIS SONS.

THEY CONTINUE THEIR JOURNEY.

WHEN Lehi moved into the wilderness he went as the Lord guided him. He was told that he would be led to a choice land, and he trusted in the Lord to be guided in the right direction.

Lehi and his company had been camping by the shore of the Red Sea for some time, when one night the Lord told Lehi to start again on his journey the next morning. He did not know which way to go, but he knew the Lord would show him, as He had done before.

The next morning when Lehi arose he saw lying on the ground near his tent door a ball made of fine brass. It was curiously formed. Inside the ball were two spindles, or needles. One of these needles pointed in the direction the people were to travel. The Lord had placed this ball by Lehi's tent door that he might use it as a guide on his journey. Lehi called this ball liahona.

As the Lord commanded, Lehi's company gathered up their property, their tents, provisions and seeds of all kinds, and started in the direction that was pointed out by the liahona, or brass ball. The reason they took seeds with them was that they might plant them in the country to which they were going. As they traveled along they camped from time to time in order to get food. While stopping at camp the men would take their bows and arrows and hunt animals, which they killed for food. In those days they did not have guns, as people have now. They used bows and arrows, and sometimes slings with which they would throw stones. They did not make fires to cook their food, but ate the meat raw. The Lord blessed the food for their sakes and it made them strong and healthy.

LEHI FINDS THE LIAHONA.

Sometimes it was hard for the men to get enough food for all the company. The animals were not very plentiful, although the road they took was through the best part of the country, along the side of the Red Sea. But much of the country through which they traveled was rocky and barren. There was but little water to be found.

At one time when the company stopped Nephi broke his bow while he and his brethren were hunting. His brothers' bows about the same time lost their springs and were not as good as they had been. On this account they returned to camp without killing any animals, and so they were left without food.

Their bows were made of steel, and they had no way of mending them when broken. As they depended on these weapons for food they felt very sorrowful when Nephi's bow was broken. The people were hungry, and they did not know what to do to get food. Laman and Lemuel and the sons of Ishmael began to complain very much. Even Lehi complained at this time, for they were all suffering for food, and it was a very hard trial to them.

At last Nephi made a bow of wood, and out of a straight stick made an arrow. He then asked his father where he should go to get food. Lehi, not knowing where to direct him, inquired of the Lord. The Lord told Lehi to look at the ball of brass which he had found near his tent door. He did so, and there on the ball was writing which told just where he should go.

Lehi and Nephi found that the ball or liahona directed them according to their faith. When they lost faith it would not direct them, but when their faith was strong it would show them where to go or what to do.

According to the directions on the ball Nephi went into the tops of the mountains to find wild animals. There he

killed enough to furnish food for all the company, and when
he returned with it they were all glad.

After this they traveled on for several days. At the
next stopping place Ishmael died, and was buried there. His
daughters mourned very much over his loss, and they
complained of Lehi for bringing them from Jerusalem.
Laman and Lemuel were still not satisfied, and they found
fault with their father, and wanted to kill him and Nephi and
then go back to their old home.

But the Lord was with Nephi. His Holy Spirit rested
upon him when he spoke to his brothers, and by reasoning
with them he pursuaded them to obey their father Lehi.

The next stopping place for this little colony or company
of people was near the shore of the Arabian Sea or Indian
Ocean, a long, long way from Jerusalem. Here was a
beautiful country in which there was to be found plenty of
food of different kinds. They named this place Bountiful,
because so much fruit and honey was found there. They
had spent eight years in the wilderness traveling between
Jerusalem and this place near the great ocean.

From this story we can learn some good lessons. It
shows us that the Lord is ever watching over His children.
When Lehi and his company were in want of food He knew
of their suffering, but He wanted to try them. When they
had been tried enough He showed them how to obtain the
food they needed. On this journey the company learned
that it was necessary to trust in the Lord and have faith in
Him, for they saw that the brass ball which was given them
by the Lord to direct them would work only according to
their faith.

————— —

Points to be remembered in this story:—Lehi instructed by the Lord
to continue on his journey—He finds a brass ball by his tent door—It
points out the direction in which the company should travel—The colony

start again on their journey—They stop at times to catch wild animals to eat—Use bows and arrows to shoot with—Nephi breaks his bow, and the company are without food—Nephi makes a wooden bow and goes to the tops of the mountain, where he finds plenty of animals—At another stopping place Ishmael dies, Laman and Lemuel want to kill Lehi and Nephi—Nephi by the power of the Lord gets them to obey their father—The company continue their travels and come to the great sea, now called the Arabian Sea, or Indian Ocean—Here they find plenty of food—The Lord always watches over His children—He lets them suffer in order to try them—It is necessary to trust in the Lord always.

LEHI AND HIS SONS.

NEPHI BUILDS A SHIP.

AFTER arriving at the place which they called Bountiful, near the great ocean, Lehi and his company pitched their tents and rested for many days. Here the Lord spoke to Nephi and told him to go to a mountain. Nephi obeyed the voice of the Lord. When he was upon the mountain he prayed, and the Lord told him he was to build a ship that the people might be carried in it across the ocean, to the land of promise.

The Lord promised Nephi that He would show him how to build this ship. Nephi had no tools with which to make a ship, and he did not know how he should get along with the work. But the Lord showed him where he might find iron ore out of which to make tools.

Nephi then made out of the skins of animals a bellows, such as blacksmiths use to blow the fire. He then made a fire by striking two stones together. He did not have matches, such as we use to make a light.

While the company were traveling in the wilderness they did not make much fire. The Lord did not desire them to make much fire or light. He caused their food to taste sweet without cooking.

NEPHI AND HIS BRETHREN BUILDING A SHIP.

This the Lord did that they might know that He was their Leader, and that it was by His power they were fed and cared for.

After making a fire, Nephi melted the iron ore to get the iron out of it, and then he made tools from the iron.

When Nephi's brothers saw that he was going to build a ship and cross the ocean in it they made fun of him and called him foolish. They did not believe he could build a ship, nor did they think he could cross the great waters in the ship if he should build one. They were not willing to help him, as they did not believe he was instructed by the Lord.

Nephi reasoned with his brethren when he found they did not believe the Lord had instructed him to build the ship. He reminded them of how the Lord delivered their forefathers out of Egypt, and how He had led their father Lehi and family from Jerusalem, and cared for them on their way. Nephi also spoke to them about their wickedness and their unbelief. This made them angry again, and they wanted to throw him into the sea. As they were about to take hold of him Nephi commanded them in the name of the Lord to not touch him. He was filled with the Spirit of the Lord, and told them if they touched him the Lord would smite them, or strike them so that they would wither.

For several days after this they did not dare to touch Nephi. Then the Lord told him to stretch his arm out towards his brethren, and He would shake them. This Nephi did and the Lord shook them so much that they were willing to believe in Him. They then fell down and were going to worship Nephi, but he told them to worship the Lord and honor their father and mother.

The brothers were now willing to help Nephi build the ship.

From time to time, as He promised, the Lord instructed Nephi about how he should make the vessel, and Nephi and

STYLES OF SHIPS USED IN OLDEN TIMES.

his brethren got out timber and worked it according to the instructions they received.

When the ship was finished they saw that it was good, and the work on it was very fine; and those who laughed at Nephi and said he could not build a ship were humble now, and they believed the Lord had guided and instructed him.

Now that the ship was built, the Lord told Lehi to take his family and all who were with him and get into it. So after preparing much fruit, and meat, and honey, and other provisions which they needed they all got into the ship, and started out on their journey or voyage.

They still had to be led by the Lord, as they did not know which way to travel. When the ship was launched or loosened from the shore the wind blew it in the direction of the land to which the Lord desired to take them.

We learn from this story that Lehi and his company were led in the wilderness much in the same way as the children of Israel were, when they left Egypt. The children of Israel were forty years in the wilderness going from Egypt to Jerusalem. The distance between these two places was not so very far. The reason they were so long in going was because the Lord desired to teach them certain lessons before they ended their journey, and it took all this time to prepare them to enter the land to which they were being led. Lehi and his company were eight years going from Jerusalem to the sea shore where they built the ship. They too, might have traveled faster, but some of them were disobedient and complained very much. They did not have patience enough and did not trust in the Lord as they should nor believe that He was leading them. The Lord wanted them to learn these things and so He caused them to remain a long time in the wilderness, where they received an experience which was valuable to them.

Points to be remembered in this story:—Nephi is commanded by the Lord to build a ship, with which to cross the ocean—He melts ore and gets iron to make tools—His brothers call him foolish and refuse to help him—He reasons with them and they try to throw him into the sea—Nephi commands them to not touch him or the Lord will smite them—The Lord shakes them; they then believe what their brother has told them and are willing to help him build a ship—When the ship is finished all the people in the company go into it and they start on their voyage—The journey of Lehi and his company was like that of the children of Israel when they left Egypt.

LEHI AND HIS SONS.

ARRIVAL ON THE PROMISED LAND.

AFTER sailing on the ocean for several days Nephi's brothers, Laman and Lemuel, and the sons of Ishmael, with their wives, began to make themselves merry. They sang, and danced, and spoke with much rudeness. They seemed by their actions to have forgotten how the Lord had cared for them and guided them through the wilderness.

Nephi was afraid their actions would offend the Lord, and he spoke to them about their behavior. But as before, this made them angry, and they said they would not be ruled over by their younger brother. Laman and Lemuel took Nephi and bound him with cords and treated him very cruelly. Nephi was bound so tightly that he could not move.

As soon as Nephi was bound the liahona, or brass ball, failed to direct them in the course they should take, and a great storm arose. The ship was driven backward for three days, and those on board began to be frightened, as they were in danger of being drowned.

But Laman and Lemuel were so wicked at heart that they would not release Nephi. Their father talked with them, but this did not soften their hearts. Lehi and Sariah his wife were getting old, and the troubles caused them by their older sons made them very sick. Their two younger sons, Jacob and Joseph, who were born in the wilderness, were much in need of their mother's care, and were grieved because of her sickness. Nephi's wife and children cried and prayed for him to be released, but this had no effect upon Laman and Lemuel. Nothing but the power of God would move them.

On the fourth day after Nephi was bound the storm became more severe, and it seemed as though the ship would sink. The storm was so terrible that Laman and Lemuel became fearful that they would be drowned. They then repented of their wicked acts and loosened the bands that held their brother.

Nephi's wrists and ankles, around which the cords were tied, were very much swollen and very sore; but he did not complain. He thanked the Lord and praised |Him for His goodness.

After being released Nephi took the brass ball, or compass, as it was also called, and it began to work again. He prayed to the Lord and the storm ceased, and the ship was guided towards the promised land.

For many days they continued to sail, and at last they reached the shore of the land of promise. The place where they landed was in the country now called Chili, in South America.

Here they got out of the ship and put up their tents. They planted the seeds which they brought with them from Jerusalem. The seeds grew, and soon they were rewarded with abundant crops.

They found that there were animals of all kinds in the forests. There were cattle, and horses, and goats, and many other animals. They also found gold, and silver, and copper.

ARRIVAL ON THE PROMISED LAND.

This was indeed the choice land to which the Lord promised to lead Lehi and his colony. Here they could live in
peace and happiness if they would keep the Lord's commandments. There were no other people in the country to
disturb them.

This story shows us that the Lord is true to His promises. Everything He promised Lehi and Nephi was fulfilled.
Laman and Lemuel, who were so full of unbelief in regard
to the Lord's promises, could now see that they were all
true.

They had no way of getting news from Jerusalem, and
they could not tell what was happening there; but the Lord
showed to Lehi in a vision the destruction of Jerusalem,
which took place just about the time his colony reached the
promised land.

Points to be remembered in this story: While in the ship Laman,
Lemuel and Ishmael's sons with their wives act rude—Nephi was not pleased
with their behavior and speaks to them—They get angry and bind Nephi
with cords—A great storm arises and nearly sinks the ship—On the fourth
day of the storm it becomes more terrible and Laman and Lemuel fear they
will be drowned and release Nephi—Nephi prays to the Lord and the storm
ceases—After sailing many days they reach the promised land—The country
they arrive at is now called Chili, in South America—They plant the seed
which they brought from Jerusalem and raise abundant crops—They find
all kinds of animals in the forests, and gold, silver and copper in the earth—
This is the choice land to which the Lord promised to lead them—The Lord
fulfills all His promises—Lehi saw the destruction of Jerusalem in a vision.

LEHI AND HIS SONS.

LEHI BLESSES HIS CHILDREN.

WHEN the little colony of people led by Lehi arrived on the promised land Lehi was quite aged. He knew that he would not live very long. Before he died he wanted to speak to his children and grandchildren and all who came with him across the great ocean. He also desired to bless them, and as he was their father and a servant of the Lord, it was his right to do so.

Lehi was a great prophet. The Lord told him many things that would happen in years to come. When he called his people together to speak to them and bless them, he told them many things which the Lord showed unto him. He reminded them of the great mercy of God in leading them to such a beautiful land, and told them that if they and their children after them would be faithful in keeping the commandments of the Lord, they should possess the land forever.

The Lord had kept this land for a good people, and as long as they should serve Him they would prosper, but when they became wicked they would not be protected by the Lord. Other people would be led to their country and take possession of it.

Lehi told what should happen to his children or posterity down to the time in which we live. He also gave them some very good instructions. These instructions you can read in the Book of Mormon when you become older. The advice or counsel he gave them is good for others as well as his children, and should be read by everyone who is able to understand it.

LEHI BLESSING HIS FAMILY.

After telling them about these things, Lehi called his children to him one by one and blessed them.

In speaking to Laman and Lemuel, Lehi said he feared very much for them. On account of their disobedience he was afraid the Lord would cause a curse to come upon them and their children. He asked them to be obedient to Nephi, their younger brother, whom the Lord promised should be their leader on account of his faithfulness and obedience. If they would do as he desired them, Lehi promised they should not perish, but if they would not, the blessings he promised them would be taken from them.

In speaking to his other sons Lehi also instructed them to listen to and obey the counsel of Nephi, and promised that their children and Nephi's children should dwell together and be one people, and that they and their children should dwell in peace in the land for a long time.

Soon after blessing his children and giving them the instructions he desired they should receive, Lehi died, and his children buried him.

If Laman and Lemuel were not so rebellious and unwilling to believe they might have seen many things to prove that their father was indeed a true prophet. Everything he prophesied about came to pass just as he said; and many of his prophecies were fulfilled while Laman and Lemuel were living. They could see and understand that the Lord spoke to their father, but they were wicked and disobedient. In following stories we will learn what happened to them for their disobedience.

Points to be remembered in this story: Before Lehi dies he calls his family together to bless them and to tell them about what will happen in years to come—He instructs them to keep the commandments of the Lord and obey the teachings of Nephi—Lehi dies—Laman and Lemuel do not believe in their father's words because of their wickedness and rebellion.

LEHI AND HIS SONS.

NEPHI AND HIS PEOPLE SEEK A NEW HOME.

NOT many days after the death of Lehi, Laman and Lemuel and the sons of Ishmael again became angry with Nephi. This was because he had counseled them as the Lord had told him, to be more faithful. Nephi desired his brethren to do better, and this was why he talked with them. He also prayed for them that their hearts might be softened. But their hearts were evil. They became more angry with Nephi and tried to take his life.

They said among themselves, "Our younger brother thinks to rule over us, and we have had much trial because of him; wherefore now let us slay him, that we may not be afflicted more because of his words. For behold we will not have him to be our ruler; for it belongs unto us who are the older brethren, to rule over this people."

They did not tell Nephi of their intention to kill him, that they might be rulers of the people. But the Lord warned him of what his brethren wanted to do, and instructed him to leave them and go into the wilderness. He was also to take with him all the people who were willing to follow him.

All those who believed in the revelations of the Lord listened to Nephi and obeyed his instructions, and they were willing to follow him into the wilderness. Among these were Nephi's family, Zoram and his family, Sam and his family and Nephi's sisters.

After traveling for many days they found a place suitable for them to dwell in, and there they pitched their tents. This place they named Nephi, after their leader whom they

THE NEPHITES SEEKING A NEW HOME.

loved. The people also called themselves the people of Nephi. From this time on for many hundreds of years these people and their children were called Nephites, and those who remained with Laman and Lemuel were called Lamanites.

The place to which Nephi led his people when they left Laman and Lemuel is believed to be north of where they landed from the ship when they first came to the promised land It was either in the country now called Ecuador or in Peru, in South America.

The Lord blessed the people who went with Nephi to build up a new home. They planted crops and raised an abundance of food. They also raised herds of cattle and other animals that were useful to them.

The Lord told Lehi that He would lead him and his children to a rich and choice land; and so it was. His promise was fulfilled, just as it always is.

When Nephi left his disobedient brethren he took with him the brass plates which they obtained from Laban in Jerusalem. The records on these plates were very valuable to him, and he desired to keep them for his children and all who should live after him. These records contained the laws and the commandments of the Lord, and Nephi and his people desired to obey these commandments.

Nephi also took with him the sword of Laban and the brass ball or liahona which his father found near his tent door while traveling in the wilderness, and which pointed out the way for him to travel. Nephi used the sword of Laban as a pattern to make other swords by. This was in order that his people might defend or protect themselves from Laman and Lemuel and those who were with them. Nephi knew that they hated him and his people and would try to kill them if they had the chance.

It was a wise thing for Nephi to have his people make swords to protect themselves with, for in less than forty years after the time they came across the sea to the promised land they had wars and contentions with the Lamanites.

We learn from this story that Laman and Lemuel wanted to rule the people, but the Lord had promised Nephi that he should be their leader on account of his faithfulness. The Lord also said that Laman and Lemuel and their children should be cut off from His presence, that is He would not speak to them or give them revelations if they did not obey Him. Nephi did become the leader of the people, and the Lamanites were shut out from receiving revelations from the Lord on account of their wickedness, showing that the Lord's words were fulfilled. We see by this that the Lord is very particular to keep every promise He makes to His servants. We should also be very careful to keep our promises to one another and to our Heavenly Father.

Points to be remembered in this story : Laman, Lemuel and Ishmael's sons get angry at Nephi and plan among themselves to kill him—The Lord warns Nephi of their intentions and tells him to leave them and go into another part of the country—Those who believe Nephi's words and teachings go with him into the wilderness to find a new home—They travel many days and settle at a place which they name Nephi after their leader—This people afterwards called Nephites, and those whom they left called Lamanites—Here they are greatly blessed of the Lord—They sow seeds and reap an abundance of food—The records on the brass plates, the brass ball and the sword of Laban taken by Nephi to his new home—Nephi makes swords for his people to defend themselves with—The Lord's promises to Nephi are fulfiled.

LEHI AND HIS SONS.

NEPHI AND HIS PEOPLE BUILD A TEMPLE.

AFTER Nephi and his people had separated themselves from Laman and his followers, the Lord placed a curse upon the Lamanites. He caused a skin of blackness to come upon them. Before this they were a white and beautiful people; but that they might not be attractive to the Nephites, the Lord caused them to appear loathsome and offensive. This was in order to keep them from associating together in any way.

The Lord instructed the Nephites to not mix with the Lamanites, and told them if they did they too would become cursed like them. The only way for the Lamanites to free themselves from their curse was to repent of their sins. After this curse came upon the Lamanites they became idle, mischievous and filthy; and they gained their living by hunting wild animals and eating their flesh.

Nephi had a great deal to do among his people. Besides teaching them the commandments of the Lord he had to instruct them about many other things. He had to teach them how to build houses, how to work wood, and iron, and copper, and brass, and steel, and gold, and silver, in order to make useful articles out of these materials. He also taught them how to obtain metals from the ore, which was found in great abundance in the mountains. He was very desirous that the people should become industrious and learn to labor with their hands.

Nephi's younger brothers, Jacob and Joseph, and his
own children and those of Sam and Zoram were born after

THE NEPHITES BUILDING A TEMPLE.

their fathers left Jerusalem. They did not know much about building or other kind of work, for they never had seen a city nor even a house. During their travels in the wilderness they lived in tents. Some of these children might have remembered seeing their parents building the ship in which they crossed the ocean, but they were very young at that time.

After teaching the people how to work at these different occupations Nephi built a temple in which the people might meet to worship the Lord and receive instructions. He had the temple made like the one in Jerusalem, which was built by King Solomon, only it was not built of so many precious things. Nephi had seen the temple in Jerusalem and knew how it was built, and he made one like it as near as he could. The work on it was very fine.

Nephi was so well beloved by his people that they desired to make him their king. He did not wish them to have a king but was willing to act as a leader and do all he could for them.

He needed some one to help him as a teacher of the people and he appointed and set apart his two younger brothers Jacob and Joseph as priests, that they might instruct the people. These two men were faithful in their duties and they gave the people very good instruction. The Lord blessed them in their labors and showed them in visions many glorious things, just as he had shown their brother Nephi.

We learn from this story that Nephi was a very wise man. He was able to teach his people how to work at different kinds of occupations as well as to instruct them in their duties to the Lord. Nephi became wise by being obedient. He was taught many things by the Lord. He prayed to the Lord to know what to do and his prayers were answered. The Lord helps those who ask for His aid. He is willing to help them in their work or in their study, or if they are in trouble, or in whatever way they need His help. The only way to be truly wise and to get correct knowledge is to seek the Lord for His guidance.

Points to be remembered in this story: After the Nephites and Lamanites separate the Lord places a curse upon the Lamanites—Causes a skin of darkness to come upon them—This was to make them loathsome to the Nephites, so that they would not associate together—The Lamanites become idle and mischievous—Nephi teaches his people how to work at different occupations—He builds a temple like the one in Jerusalem—The people love Nephi and want to make him their king—He does not wish them to have a king but is willing to do all he can for them as a leader and teacher—Nephi appoints his brothers Jacob and Joseph as priests to help him teach the people their duties—Nephi a wise man—Becomes wise by being obedient to the Lord.

LEHI AND HIS SONS.

NEPHI MAKES PLATES ON WHICH TO KEEP A RECORD.

NEPHI was very particular to keep a record or history of his people, and to record the instructions he received from the Lord. This was in order that the people might know the many great things the Lord had done for them and their forefathers.

The Lord was very particular about Nehi taking a record of his forefathers with him when he left Jerusalem. You will remember that Nephi and his brothers were sent to Laban for the records, and Nephi was commanded of the Lord to kill Laban in order to get them. The Lord knew that by having the people keep a record of His dealings with them they would not be so apt to forget Him and His commandments.

The Book of Mormon tells about a company of people who left Jerusalem eleven years later than did Nehi and his colony. They brought no records with·them. A little more than three hundred years later the children or descendants of these people were found by the people of Nephi. At this time their langnage was corrupted or changed so much that the two peoples could not understand each other. These people who were without records of any kind had also lost all knowledge of the Lord. They did not know there was a God. This shows how important it is that records should be kept so that the people may remember the commandments of the Lord, and not forget Him as these people did.

Nephi made some plates from metal on which he wrote or engraved an account of his people from the time they left Jerusalem until a short time before he died. On these plates he wrote a full history of the people. Afterwards the Lord told him to make other plates and engrave upon them certain instructions for the benefit of his people.

When Nephi became old he gave the plates which contained the records to his brother Jacob and instructed him about what to write on them. Jacob in turn when he grew old gave them to his son. In this way the history of the people was kept for many hundreds of years.

Next to the last man among the Nephites who had charge of the records was one named Mormon. Besides writing an account of what happened in his own time, Mormon made from these records which were on the plates a short history of the people from the days of Lehi to his own time. This history which he wrote is what was translated by Joseph Smith. It is called the Book of Mormon because it

was written by Mormon.   His son whose name was Moroni
was the last man among the Nephites who wrote on the

NEPHI MAKING PLATES.

plates.   He was also the last prophet that lived among them.
When he finished the history the people were fighting and
killing each other.   They had become wicked and would not
obey the commandments of the Lord nor listen to the instructions of His servants the prophets.   On this account the
Lord allowed them to destroy each other.   His prophets
Lehi and Nephi said they would be destroyed if they would
not serve the Lord.

When Moroni finished writing the history of the
Nephites he placed the plates containing the records in a
stone box and buried them in a hill.   With the plates he also
placed in the box the sword of Laban which Nephi took to
slay Laban with and a gold breastplate such as the people
used to protect themselves in war; also the urim and thummim, or interpreters.

This stone box and its contents remained in the ground
where it was buried fourteen hundred years.   On the 22nd
day of September, 1827, this same man Moroni, who had
died and was resurrected, or raised to life again, showed
Joseph Smith the Prophet where this stone box was buried,
and gave him permission to take the plates and other things
out.

With the urim and thummim or interpreters, Joseph
Smith translated or changed the writings on some of the
plates into the English language.   In this way the Book of
Mormon was given to the people who live in our time.   The
urim and thummim was two precious stones fastened into a
silver rim.   They had been prepared by the Lord·for the
purpose of translating.   By looking on these stones the
Prophet Joseph Smith could see the English words to be
written for the words which were engraved on the plates.

When Nephi became old and knew that he would soon
die he anointed a man to be king to rule over the people

He had already appointed his brothrs Jacob and Joseph as priets to instruct them in their duties to the Lord. He himself had taught them many things about religion and other matters, and now he was prepared to die. He lived a good life, having been faithful in doing everything the Lord commanded him.

———

Points to be remembered in this story: Nephi kept a record of his people so they might remember what the Lord had done for them—If they did not have the Lord's commandments written they would easily forget them—Nephi makes plates of metal on which to write the history of his people—These plates were given by one man to another to keep for many hundreds of years—Moroni the next to last man who wrote on the plates copied a short history of the people from them which is called the Book of Mormon—Moroni, Mormon's son finished the records and hid them in a stone box—Fourteen hundred years afterwards Moroni showed Joseph Smith where the plates were hidden, and gave him permission to take them out of the ground—With the urim and thummim Joseph Smith translated the writings on some of the plates—Before he died Nephi anointed a man to be king over the people.

www.ingramcontent.com/pod-product-compliance
Lightning Source LLC
Chambersburg PA
CBHW031800090426
42739CB00008B/1095

* 9 7 8 3 3 3 7 2 9 8 3 7 1 *